A HEART
for
God

A HEART
for
God

JULIE ACKERMAN LINK

DISCOVERY HOUSE

PUBLISHERS

A Heart for God
© 2010 by Julie Ackerman Link
All rights reserved.

Discovery House Publishers is affiliated with RBC Ministries,
Grand Rapids, Michigan.

Discovery House books are distributed to the trade exclusively by
Barbour Publishing, Inc., Uhrichsville, Ohio.

Requests for permission to quote from this book should be directed to:
Permissions Department, Discovery House Publishers, P.O. Box 3566,
Grand Rapids, MI 49501.

Scripture quotations are taken from the Holy Bible, New International
Version®. NIV®. Copyright © 1973, 1978, 1984 by Biblica, Inc.™ Used by
permission of Zondervan. All rights reserved worldwide. www.zondervan.com

A Heart for God is based on the concepts developed in *Above All, Love: Reflections
on the Greatest Commandment*, © 2008 by Julie Ackerman Link.

Lesson 13 is adapted from the introduction, written by the author, for the
book *Faith: A Holy Walk* by Oswald Chambers, © 1999, Oswald Chambers
Publications Association, Limited.

Library of Congress Cataloging-in-Publication Data available upon request.

Printed in the United States of America

10 11 12 13 14 15 16 17 / CHG / 10 9 8 7 6 5 4 3 2 1

CONTENTS

Space is provided throughout the book for answering questions, but some readers may want to use an additional notebook or journal to have more room for interacting with the ideas and questions.

WHEN I STARTED studying the Greatest Commandment, I slowly came to realize that nearly all of life's problems are due to the fact that each aspect of our being—heart, soul, mind, and strength—is completely out of alignment with God. The damage started shortly after creation at the event called "the fall," and it continues to this day because of ongoing disobedience. As a result, we are in conflict not only with God, but also with ourselves and others.

The apostle Paul gave the clearest biblical description of this condition that I have found:

> So I find this law at work: When I want to do good, evil is right there with me. For in my inner being I delight in God's law; but I see another law at work in the members of my body, waging war against the law of my mind and making me a prisoner of the law of sin at work within my members. What a wretched man I am! Who will rescue me from this body of death? Thanks be to God—through Jesus Christ our Lord! (Romans 7:21–25)

He wrote something similar to believers living in Asia:

> [T]he sinful nature desires what is contrary to the Spirit,
> and the Spirit what is contrary to the sinful nature. They
> are in conflict with each other, so that you do not do what
> you want. (Galatians 5:17)

James elaborated on the idea:

> What causes fights and quarrels among you? Don't they
> come from your desires that battle within you? You want
> something but don't get it. You kill and covet, but you
> cannot have what you want. You quarrel and fight. You
> do not have, because you do not ask God. When you
> ask, you do not receive, because you ask with wrong
> motives, that you may spend what you get on your
> pleasures. (James 4:1–3)

The problem, as these and other Scriptures indicate, is that we want what God says isn't good for us; we try to be someone other than who God created us to be; we think wrongly about God, ourselves, and others; and we use our strength to satisfy ourselves rather than glorify God.

Our only hope is to recognize our condition, to be reconciled to God through Christ, and to allow Him to recreate and realign us until we once again reflect His glory for all the world to see. This will happen when we learn to love God with all our heart, soul, mind, and strength. Then, and only then, will we also be able to love ourselves and our neighbors.

HELP!

I've Fallen and I Can't Get Up

Genesis 2–3; Romans 7:14–25; 16:17–20

THE FALL OF Adam sent curators at New York's Metropolitan Museum of Art to their knees. But they weren't repenting of the sin that started in the garden of Eden with the fall of the first Adam. They were lamenting the plunge of a priceless fifteenth-century sculpture from its pedestal, and they were on their knees picking up the fragments.

When the statue fell, it didn't break into nice neat pieces. The arms, legs, and head separated from the torso in such a way that they could not be glued back together easily. In the words of one restorer, part of Adam was "pulverized." Experts predicted that it would take two years to piece Adam together again, but they promised he would be almost as good as new by the time he was returned to public view.

Imagine if you were given the dust and particles of Adam and were told to put him back together again. How long do you think it would take? What do you think Adam would look like when you were finished?

Now imagine if the dust tried to reshape itself.

That's what we attempt to do whenever we try to "restore" ourselves from the effects of the fall. Like the statue, the original Adam and everyone after him has been shattered and pulverized by sin. We all lie in a pile of dust on the floor of creation—splintered emotions, pulverized personality, twisted minds, and broken bodies. And we have only one hope for wholeness—the One who created us. He alone has the knowledge and skill to put us back together.

In Scripture, the categories of heart, soul, mind, and strength are not precise divisions; there is much overlap. For example, the Bible sometimes indicates that thinking happens in the heart (e.g., Zechariah 7:10; Mark 2:8). For the purpose of this study, however, we will use heart, soul, mind, and strength to refer to the following:

Heart	Desires, emotions, feelings
Soul	Being, identity, life, self
Mind	Beliefs, discernment, knowledge, thoughts, truth
Strength	Actions, boldness, courage, enthusiasm, intensity, obedience

LESSON ONE: *Help!*

1. Read Genesis 3. What tactics did Satan use to get the woman to eat the fruit God had forbidden (vv. 1–5)?

    Using the following category descriptions, what appeals did Satan make to her *heart*, *soul*, *mind*, or *strength*?

Heart	**Soul**	**Mind**	**Strength**
Desires	*Being*	*Beliefs*	*Actions*
Emotions	*Identity*	*Discernment*	*Boldness*
Feelings	*Life*	*Knowledge*	*Courage*
	Self	*Thoughts*	*Enthusiasm*
		Truth	*Intensity*
			Obedience

2. Compare the discussion between Eve and the Serpent (Genesis 3:1–5) with what God really said to Adam (2:15–18). How do the two accounts differ? Since Eve was created *after* the command was given (v. 18), what can we assume about her knowledge of what God said?

3. Why did Eve disobey God (Genesis 3:6)?

4. What knowledge did Adam and Eve gain (3:7)?

5. What did this new information cause them to do (3:7–8)?

6. Instead of angrily confronting them with their wrongdoing, how did God respond (3:9–13)?

7. How did Adam and Eve defend themselves (3:9–13)?

Lesson One: *Help!*

8. The curse on Eve (3:16) involved her desires. How does this correspond to her sin (3:6)? What did Eve want that she wasn't supposed to have?

9. The curse on Adam involved his work (3:17–19). How does this correspond to his sin (3:6b)? Whose job was it to guard the tree (2:15–17)?

Fast forward to the first century: The second Adam (Christ) has come to heal our brokenness. However, all is not yet well. Conflicts continue. We are divided not only *from* one another but *within* ourselves. The apostle Paul wrote a classic description of this inner turmoil. Read Romans 7:14–25. Using the following chart as a guide, make a list of all the words in this passage that relate to *heart*, *soul*, *mind*, and *strength*.

Heart	**Soul**	**Mind**	**Strength**
Desires	Being	Beliefs	Actions
Emotions	Identity	Discernment	Boldness
Feelings	Life	Knowledge	Courage
	Self	Thoughts	Enthusiasm
		Truth	Intensity
			Obedience

10. Do you have an internal battle raging between your thoughts and desires? Are you fighting a desire to do something that your mind tells you is wrong? Or are you resisting a conviction to do something that you know is good but don't want to do? Describe the battle. What do you *want* the outcome to be?

11. Read Romans 16:17–20. Reread Genesis 3:5 and compare it with Romans 16:20. Here or in your journal write a prayer based on these passages.

May God complete His work of transformation in our lives by reversing the effects of the fall and making us wise about what is good and innocent about what is evil. Amen.

RESTORATION
The Tedious Process Begins

Deuteronomy 5–6; Numbers 15:37–41; Jeremiah 31:33;
1 Peter 3:14–15

RESTORATION HARDWARE IS one of my favorite stores. Repackaged products from the past—simple tools, toys, home decorations, and cleaning products—make me long for the beauty and simplicity of former times while leading me to believe that I can purchase the experience. But getting back to the basics of a simple life requires more than simple products, and more than a minor lifestyle readjustment. It requires a complete renovation of values.

After all, restoration doesn't begin with something new; it starts with getting rid of the old. Restoring an old house requires stripping away years of "improvements" made by previous owners who had preferences and purposes quite different from those of the original architect. Sometimes restoration involves peeling off layers of wallpaper or floor covering, but often it requires structural demolition like tearing down walls.

Getting back to the beauty of the designer's original work of art

15

is a slow, tedious process, but the satisfaction of having a house restored to its original splendor is well worth the time and effort.

God began His restoration of humans by stripping away the accumulated effects of their self-improvement projects. And He started the process with one small group of people in one small spot on planet Earth.

People sometimes question why the majority of the Ten Commandments are stated in the negative: "you shall *not* . . ." Why wasn't God more positive? Why didn't He simply tell us what *to* do instead of what *not* to do? Perhaps the reason is that God first had to strip away layers of destructive habits and behaviors the people had accumulated over the years in their misguided attempts to improve on His design.

1. Read Deuteronomy 5. With whom did God make His covenant (5:3)?

2. How did the Lord speak to the people (5:4–5)?

3. How did God identify himself (5:6)?

Lesson Two: *Restoration*

4. How did the LORD communicate the commandments (5:22)?

5. How did the people respond (5:23–27)?

6. What was the LORD's assessment of their response (5:28)?

7. What was the LORD's desire for His people (5:29)? Why?

8. In the short span of eight verses, the phrase "so that" is used five times. What do the "so thats" tell us about why God wants us to be obedient (5:29, 33; 6:2–3)?

9. Read the Ten Commandments (5:7–21) like a David Letterman Top Ten List (i.e., in reverse order). If God had written them this way (i.e., making the tenth commandment first) how many of the others would be unnecessary. In other words, how many of the commandments involve wanting something that isn't ours?

Consider: In the beginning there was only one law: "Do not eat from the tree of the knowledge of good and evil." By the time the Israelites were delivered from slavery in Egypt, more laws were needed, so God gave them the Ten Commandments. But even those were not enough. The book of Leviticus records more laws. Arranged in categories of civil, ceremonial, and moral, they elaborated on the original ten.

Compare this to our own legal system. In our system of justice, laws are added as people find new ways to behave badly, often in the form of taking what doesn't belong to them or endangering something that belongs to someone else. This gives credence to the idea that *breaking* the law doesn't *make* us sinners but that *being* sinners we are in need of laws.

For further study, read what Jesus said about the Sabbath being made for man, not vice versa (Matthew 12:1–8). In other words, the law is for our good. Breaking the law doesn't *make* us bad (we already are); the law just helps us know what is good.

"We know that the law is good if one uses it properly. We also know that law is made not for the righteous but for lawbreakers and rebels, the ungodly and sinful, the unholy and irreligious;

for those who kill their fathers or mothers, for murderers, for adulterers and perverts, for slave traders and liars and perjurers—and for whatever else is contrary to the sound doctrine that conforms to the glorious gospel of the blessed God, which he entrusted to me." (1 Timothy 1:8–11)

10. Read Deuteronomy 6. The Jews refer to verses 4–5 as *Shema*.

> "The *Shema* is a declaration of faith, a pledge of allegiance to One God. It is said upon arising in the morning and upon going to sleep at night. It is said when praising God and when beseeching Him. It is the first prayer that a Jewish child is taught to say. It is the last words a Jew says prior to death." (Rabbi Shraga Simmons)

What important statement does *Shema* make about God? What is unique about the God of Israel (6:4)?

How were the people to love God (6:5)?

Why do you think God made distinctions between *heart*, *soul*, and *strength*?

Moses had just emphasized that God is one (i.e., integrated in all aspects of His being), so what might he have been saying about God's intention for those who love Him?

Would you characterize your love for God as being more emotional, intellectual, or experiential? What might be different if you focused for a while on loving God in the area in which your love is weak?

11. What memory devices were the Jews to use to keep them from forgetting these commands (Deuteronomy 6:6–9; Numbers 15:37–41)?

How can we adapt this concept to our own culture? What contemporary examples can you think of?

Read Jeremiah 31:31–33. What happened to the people's obedience?

What practices do we follow only outwardly, with our bodies, without engaging our hearts and minds?

The display of the Ten Commandments in public buildings has been known to generate controversy. In what safe place does God want His commands to exist so they cannot be banned by any government?

12. Why might eating and being satisfied cause someone to forget God (Deuteronomy 6:10–12)?

13. What does Deuteronomy 6:13–15 say about the emotional nature of God? How does God's warning relate to the first and tenth commandments?

14. Compare Deuteronomy 6:20–25 with 1 Peter 3:14–15. In the following chart, list the allusions in these verses to matters of *heart*, *soul*, *mind*, and *strength*.

Heart	Soul	Mind	Strength
Desires	*Being*	*Beliefs*	*Actions*
Emotions	*Identity*	*Discernment*	*Boldness*
Feelings	*Life*	*Knowledge*	*Courage*
	Self	*Thoughts*	*Enthusiasm*
		Truth	*Intensity*
			Obedience

15. What is the reason for your hope?

16. Consider this quotation by Susan Lenzkes: "God . . . wants your whole heart, even if it comes to Him in broken, jagged pieces."

How has your heart been broken? How is God working to restore it? In what ways is God trying to make you one with himself in *heart*, *soul*, *mind*, and *strength*?

17. Write a prayer of response to God.

DESIRE
Wanting What God Wants

2 Chronicles 1; 1 Chronicles 28; Mark 10:35–52; James 4:1–3

"WHEN PEOPLE LOOK inside your car or closet, do they see any evidence that you believe in a God who brings order out of chaos?"

I hate that question. I've hated it since the day I heard it at a college retreat. But I hate the answer even more. I don't like having to acknowledge that the answer is "No."

Answering the question causes both guilt and anxiety. The guilt comes from the belief that God hates my disorderly ways. The anxiety comes from the fear that maybe God also hates me. In trying to reconcile the way this makes me feel about myself with the truth I know about God, I've discovered two points of view.

Some people say that I just need to try harder; God wants me to be neat, so if I want it badly enough I will be. So I try binge cleaning. When I get everything in place I feel proud of myself. But only for a while. Within hours the mess is back. Like Pigpen in the *Peanuts* comic strip, I am followed by a cloud of debris. I am still a magnet for messiness.

Others say that being messy is part of being creative and I should just accept myself. God made me this way, so I might as well stop trying to be neat. I begin rationalizing that being messy is just an innocuous character trait, not an insidious defect. And I feel better about myself. But only for a while. My mind still knows that being messy is not a good way to live.

The tension mounts. If I follow the first advice, I'm in danger of becoming like the Pharisees, who led perfectly ordered lives but neglected the filth of greed and wickedness in their hearts. If I follow the second advice, I'm in danger of becoming like the pagans, who led undisciplined lives because they failed to distinguish between good and bad, clean and unclean.

Praise God, there's a third alternative. More important than keeping a clean car or a clean closet is having a clean heart. Jesus put it this way: "First clean the inside . . . and then the outside also will be clean" (Matthew 23:26).

The most important question I need to ask then is not, "What does the condition of my car say to the world about God?" It's "What does the condition of my heart say to God about me?"

What I want the most reveals the condition of my heart.

Lesson Three: *Desire*

1. Read 2 Chronicles 1. If God asked you the question He asked Solomon (v. 7), how would you answer?

2. How did Solomon answer (1:8–10)?

3. Why was God pleased (1:11)?

4. How did God respond to Solomon's prayer (1:12)?

5. What advice had Solomon's father, David, given to his son (1 Chronicles 28:9–10)? How does this advice relate to *heart*, *soul*, *mind*, and *strength*?

6. **Fast forward to the first century:** As Jesus and the disciples made their way to Jerusalem just before Jesus was arrested,

there were two occasions when Jesus asked the question, "What do you want me to do for you?"

Read Mark 10:35–45. When asked the question, what did James and John answer (v. 37)?

What selfish or unreasonable requests do we sometimes make of God?

In what ways has God protected you from your unwise requests?

7. Instead of scolding them for their selfishness, how did Jesus answer (Mark 10:38–39)?

8. How did the other disciples respond when they heard what James and John had requested (Mark 10:41)?

What happens when our desires conflict with God's (James 4:1–3)?

9. Seizing this "teachable moment," Jesus gave His disciples a lesson about their wants and desires. What was it (Mark 10:42–45)?

How does this change your attitude about power and authority?

10. Review Deuteronomy 6:7. In what ways did Jesus demonstrate how to obey this command?

11. As Jesus and His disciples approached Jericho, a blind man heard that He was coming, and he began to shout, "Jesus, Son of David, have mercy on me!" (Mark 10:47). Jesus asked this man the same question He asked James and John: "What do you want me to do for you?" What did the man answer (v. 51)?

It is surprising that Jesus had to ask what the man wanted because the answer seems obvious. Read James 4:1–3 again. What does it say about the importance of asking?

12. In Gethsemane, just before being arrested, Jesus was praying not for himself, but for us. What did He want for us (John 17:20–26)?

13. Go back to question #1. Having completed the study, would you answer it differently? If so, in what way?

14. What steps could you take this week to align your desires, feelings, and emotions with God's?

15. Read Psalm 23 in a translation other than the one you usually use. Try reading it as if you've never heard it before. What does it say about "want"?

LESSON THREE: *Desire*

How does this relate to the tenth commandment (from the previous lesson)?

List the ways that this psalm addresses matters of the heart — desires, feelings, and emotions.

16. Choose one of the following options.

• Rewrite Psalm 23 in your own words.
• Read Psalm 40:8 and Psalm 63. Use one as a basis for a personal prayer.

If you want what you have,

you will always have what you want.

If, however, you want what you don't have,

you'll never have what you want!

—Rabbi Avi Geller

NOTES

Pain

Feeling the Sting of Sin and Death

Genesis 6; Hosea 11; Psalm 119:65–72; Ephesians 4:17–24;
Matthew 23; Romans 12:9–21; Psalm 118:26–27;
Luke 19:41–44; Hebrews 4:15

WHERE I LIVE, "Choose Life" bumper stickers are common. But a variation of that slogan caught my attention. It said, "Choose to Feel."

As I continued driving, I noticed that the billboards I was passing were urging me to do the opposite. They wanted me to choose things that would prevent me from feeling—alcohol to deaden emotional pain; fat-laden food to alleviate feelings of emptiness; luxury cars, diamonds, and other expensive items to lessen feelings of worthlessness.

Many of the temptations that lure us away from God do so by promising to relieve the emotional hurt we all feel due to the consequences of sin—our own or someone else's.

But God sets a different example. Instead of becoming numb or indifferent to the sting of sin, He lets us see and hear Him suffering the results of it. In one striking example, God expresses His pain in

31

terms of a parent grieving over a wayward child. "My heart churns within Me; My sympathy is stirred" (Hosea 11:8 NKJV). When we choose to feel the full range of our emotions, even grief and sadness, we come to a fuller understanding of the God who created us in His image—the image of one who feels.

It's okay to feel bad that all is not right in the world. God does too!

1. Read Genesis 6. What had happened to the human race?

What caused God's heart to be filled with pain (vv. 5–6)?

2. What was different about Noah (6:8–9)?

3. Read Hosea 11. What efforts did God make to reach out to Israel (vv. 1–4)?

4. How did Israel respond to God's kindness (11:2–3)?

5. Israel misunderstood God's discipline and failed to recognize His repeated attempts to help them. What did God want, and what did Israel refuse to do (11:5)?

"[Hosea 11, verses 8–11] are like a window into the heart of God. They show that his love for his people is a love that will never let them go." (*Zondervan NIV Bible Commentary*)

6. What aroused God's compassion (11:8)? Have you ever felt like this about one of your own children or someone else whom you love?

7. What does God say about himself and His emotions? What did He refuse to do (11:9)?

8. Read Psalm 119:65–72. When was the psalmist "afflicted" and how did affliction change his life (v. 67)?

How does this psalm characterize the arrogant? What is the condition of their hearts (119:69–70)?

What else does this psalm say about affliction (119:71)?

"Comfort and prosperity have never enriched the world as adversity has done. Out of pain and problems have come the sweetest songs, the most poignant poems, the most gripping stories. Out of suffering and tears have come the greatest spirit and the most blessed lives." (Billy Graham)

9. **Fast forward to the first century:** Read Ephesians 4:17–19. According to the apostle Paul, what happens to those who harden their hearts and lose the ability to feel?

Lesson Four: *Pain*

10. Read Matthew 23. Jesus had some harsh things to say about Israel's religious officials. He obviously was not pleased with their leadership. Listed below are some of the behaviors that grieved Him. Put a check mark in the category that seems most appropriate to you. (The purpose of this question is not to find the "right" answer, but to get you thinking about how sin permeates our lives and leaves no part untouched.)

	HEART	SOUL	MIND	STRENGTH
They did not practice what they preached (v. 3).				
They made people work hard while doing nothing themselves (v. 4).				
They made a big show out of all their righteous acts (v. 5).				
They wanted special treatment (v. 6).				
They considered themselves more important than others (vv. 6–12).				
They kept people out of God's kingdom (vv. 13–15).				
They complicated the law with their own private interpretations (v. 16).				

	Heart	Soul	Mind	Strength
They perverted the truth with their complex system of oaths (vv. 16–22).				
They emphasized the laws that benefited themselves (like tithing), but neglected those that benefited others, and which Jesus said were more important (like justice, mercy and faithfulness) (v. 23).				
They were full of greed and self-indulgence (v. 25).				
They were more concerned about looking good than being good (vv. 27–28).				
They claimed to be better than their fore-fathers (v. 30)				
They honored the prophets of the past while plotting to kill the most important prophet of all (vv. 29–34).				

11. Read Romans 12:9–21. This passage lists characteristics of

the kingdom of heaven that Christ brought to earth. Compare it to the behaviors mentioned above and list several of the ways that Christ's kingdom differs from the one the religious leaders had established.

What is God's plan for overcoming evil (12:17–21)?

12. Read Luke 19:28–44. Everyone was happy but Jesus. What made Jesus sad?

Jesus knew what was to come. The following week was going to look more like failure than success. After three years of teaching about the kingdom of heaven, Jesus knew that most people still did not understand.

People cheered because they thought Jesus was coming as king to rescue the holy city from Gentile occupation and domination. Jesus wept because they welcomed Him for the wrong reason. He had come as Savior to rescue them from the sin dominating their hearts and minds. The people rejoiced because they thought Christ's work was just beginning; Jesus mourned because He knew it was ending—even though there was much yet to be done, including the most important part.

Think about what it's like to be sad when everyone else is happy. Romans 12:15 says that we should rejoice with those who rejoice and mourn with those who mourn. The triumphal entry marked a time when the followers of Jesus were rejoicing while Jesus himself was mourning. Think of some occasions that we celebrate while God mourns, or vice versa. (See, for example, Matthew 5:11–12.)

13. Read Hebrews 4:15. How do we know that Jesus feels what we feel?

Why is it important for us to feel what Jesus feels?

PLEASURE
Delighting in God's Goodness

2 Corinthians 1:3–7; Deuteronomy 8; 16:15; Ecclesiastes 5:18–20;
Ephesians 4:28; 1 Thessalonians 4:11; Amos 8:4–6; Mark 2:27;
Exodus 23:12; Hebrews 4:10–11; Ephesians 5:1–2; Colossians 3;
James 1:19–21; 2 Corinthians 5:16–21; Deuteronomy 12:7;
Habakkuk 3:16–19; 1 Chronicles 16:10; 2 Chronicles 6:41;
Psalm 112:1

EAT WHAT YOU want and lose weight. Promises like this clutter the covers of women's magazines month after month. And women want to believe them. We want to believe that there is an easy, painless way to have the perfect body. Give us a plan, and we will eagerly follow it—at least for a day or two, maybe even a week.

But if these diets work so well, why do we need a new one every month in every magazine? And why do so many of us continue our battle of the bulge year after year?

The truth is, the only way to eat what we want and lose weight is to *want* what causes weight loss. In other words, our desires have to change before diets will work. The desire to be thin is not enough; we must also desire what will make us thin—nutritious foods and plenty of exercise.

This is not welcome information. We don't *want* to change our desires; we want our desires satisfied!

The desire to feel satisfied leads us to believe that feeling hunger is bad, so we look for eating programs that guarantee weight loss without nagging hunger pangs or rude growling sounds.

Hunger, however, is an ally, not an enemy. Hunger keeps us alive. God created it for a purpose and uses it for our good, both physically and spiritually.

Hunger reminds us of our need for God, and having hunger satisfied reminds us to be grateful. In the twisted economy of sin, however, food is thought of as a reward for good behavior or hard work rather than as an expression of God's love and care for those He created.

"Food is killing us in so many ways," said Amy Wilensky, author of *The Weight of It*, in an interview on the Diane Rehm radio program. People are using food to slowly commit suicide with one of two extremes. By either stuffing or starving ourselves, we use the good provision that God gives to sustain life in ways that actually take our lives instead. What God intended to make us strong makes us weak when used inappropriately—too much, too little, too sweet, too fat. Each of these springs from desire gone awry. What God meant for good, we use for harm.

Those who love God with all their hearts know that God's highest desire is our highest good. Therefore, we delight in all the good that God has planned for us.

1. Read 2 Corinthians 1:3–7. What does the apostle Paul say to assure us that God cares about our emotional well-being?

   God doesn't simply want to mitigate our suffering; He wants to infuse our lives with joy. In fact, enjoyment was part of His plan for creation.

God wants us to enjoy His provision.

2. Read Deuteronomy 8. What were God's purposes in taking the people through the desert to get them to the Promised Land (v. 2, 16)?

3. Why did God cause the people to hunger (8:3)?

4. What is more important than food (8:3)?

5. I grew up thinking that God was stern and difficult to please,

but I was wrong. God's detailed guidelines are given to us not simply so that we will know what pleases Him, but because He alone knows what is good for us and what will ultimately please us. Read verses 5–9 as if you've never read them before. Keep in mind that the word *discipline* also means "instruct" or "teach." What, then, is the proper purpose of discipline (8:6)?

6. What instructions are given in verse 6?

7. In verse 7, the first word, *For*, indicates that what follows is the reason for what came before (i.e., verse 6). What then is God saying about *why* we should walk in His ways?

8. What does God desire to give His people (8:7–9)?

9. What inherent danger lies in receiving so much goodness from God (8:10–14)?

What wrong conclusion are people likely to make when they are the recipients of God's bountiful blessing (8:17)?

What is wrong with this thinking (8:18) and what will be the result of it (8:19–20)?

God wants us to enjoy work and rest.

Work was part of creation *before* the fall. Work is a blessing, not a curse, and God's desire for each of us is to have meaningful work that matches our gifts and abilities and makes an important contribution to the world.

10. Read Deuteronomy 16:15. What does God say about work?

Read Ecclesiastes 5:18–20. What does Solomon say about work?

Read Ephesians 4:28 and 1 Thessalonians 4:11. What does
the apostle Paul say about work?

Even though work, like food, is good, it too has an inherent
danger. The results and rewards of work can make us feel that
our work is more important than God's. So God ordained a
Sabbath day of rest to remind us that we are dependent on His
work, not vice versa. Sadly, many have come to think of rest
as just another restriction imposed by a demanding God rather
than as a gift from a loving Father who knows what is good for
His children.

11. Read Amos 8:4–6. The people had come to think of their work
    as being more important than God's Sabbath. What else do
    people do when work and commerce become so important?
    How do they treat other people?

12. For whom was Sabbath created (Mark 2:27)?

13. In addition to humans, who (what) benefits from Sabbath rest
    (Exodus 23:12)?

14. Read Hebrews 4:9–11. How important is rest to God?

Consider: In saying "It is finished," Jesus rested from His work and let His Father finish it.

God wants us to enjoy one another.

God created Eve so that Adam would have a companion. For us to live fully and completely, we need to be engaged in peaceful, harmonious relationships with others and with Him. Many times, however, due to such human weaknesses as selfishness and pride, we break the peace. So God's gift to us includes guidelines not only for maintaining peace but also for restoring peace.

15. Read the following passages and summarize the advice they give about getting along with one another and living in peace:

2 Corinthians 5:16–21

Ephesians 5:1–2

Colossians 3 (especially verses 12–14)

James 1:19–21

God wants us to enjoy Him.

The Westminster Catechism states that the chief and highest end for all people "is to glorify God, and fully to enjoy Him forever." This goes against the thinking of those who believe that God is a spoilsport who wants to squelch everything that is fun by arbitrarily labeling it "sin." On the contrary, over and over in Scripture, God declares that He desires our enjoyment.

16. Read Deuteronomy 12:7. What are we to enjoy?

    Where?

    With whom?

    Why?

17. Read Habakkuk 3:16–19. What did the prophet enjoy?

18. Who has reason to rejoice (1 Chronicles 16:10)?

19. In what do "saints" rejoice (2 Chronicles 6:41)?

20. God knows us so well that He can foresee the results of our behavior. He knows that much of what we think will make us happy will bring misery instead, so He provides guidance to help us avoid the grief that inevitably results from bad choices.

    Read Psalm 112:1. What does it mean to "delight" in God's commands?

21. God planned feasts and celebrations into the yearly calendar of the nation of Israel. There were seven major holidays, some lasting as long as a week, and three of them were to be celebrated in one giant gathering in Jerusalem. Like rest, worship was not a duty demanded by a needy god, but a delight planned by a loving and giving God. How does it change your thoughts and feelings about God when you think of Him as someone who delights in our pleasure and enjoyment rather than as someone who wants to abolish everything that's fun?

Consider: God loves us with all His heart by placing us in a world filled with beauty and pleasure—all waiting for us to enjoy at no cost. Here or in a journal, write a psalm of praise. (Suggestion: pick a psalm to use as a sample—e.g., Psalm 16, 92, or 147.)

DEVOTION
Loving What God Loves

Psalm 11:7; 33:5; Deuteronomy 6:4–5; Matthew 22:36–40;
Romans 3:21–24; 10:1–4; Psalm 37:21; Exodus 25:2; 35:21;
1 Chronicles 29; Deuteronomy 8:10–17; Isaiah 29:13;
Mark 7:1–23; John 3:16; Romans 5:8

MAGGIE DOESN'T CARE for television. She'd rather look out a window than stare at a small screen. Reading doesn't thrill her either. She's been known to "chew" on books, but only in the strictly literal sense. Nevertheless, when Jay and I read or watch television, Maggie participates. Even though she doesn't enjoy what we're doing, she enjoys being with us. Maggie is our very devoted dog. More than anything (well, just about anything) Maggie wants to be with us.

The word "dogged" means determined and persistent. These words describe Maggie. They should also describe us. When we're devoted to God, we want to be with Him even when He's doing something that makes no sense to us. We may ask, "Why, Lord?" when He seems angry (Psalm 88:14–16), or when He seems to be napping (44:23), or when the wicked prosper (Jeremiah 12:1). But when we remain devoted to God despite our questions, we find fullness of joy in His presence (Psalm 16:11).

Even when God's ways are inexplicable, His love is reliable, which is why we should remain doggedly devoted to Him.

1. What does God love (Psalm 11:7; 33:5)?

2. Read the following definition of righteousness:

"Righteousness is . . . 'any conformity to a standard whether that standard has to do with the inner character of a person, or the objective standard of accepted law.' [J.H.] Thayer suggests the definition, 'the state of him who is such as he ought to be.' In the wide sense, it refers to that which is upright or virtuous, displaying integrity, purity of life, and correctness in feeling and action . . . [T]he Biblical approach preeminently concerns itself with the man whose way of thinking, feeling, and acting is wholly conformed to the righteousness of God." (A. H. Leitch, *Zondervan Pictorial Encyclopedia of the Bible*)

In what ways does this definition coincide with the idea

expressed in *Shema* (Deuteronomy 6:4–5; Matthew 22:36–40)?

What is the relationship between God's love for justice and what Jesus called the second greatest commandment?

3. Read Romans 3:21–24. Where does righteousness come from?

Read Romans 10:1–4. What was wrong with the zeal of the Israelites (v. 2)?

What did they misunderstand about righteousness (10:2–4)?

4. Read Psalm 37:21. What is one characteristic of the righteous?

5. What characterized the giving of the early Israelites (Exodus 25:2; 35:21)?

6. Read 1 Chronicles 29. What did David give for the building of the temple (vv. 1–5)?

   What did David ask of others (29:5)?

7. What was the result of his request (29:6–8)?

8. Why did the people rejoice (29:9)?

9. David praised the LORD in the presence of the whole assembly. What did he say about God (29:10–12)?

10. In reality, what is the only thing we have to give to God (29:13)?

11. What rhetorical question did David ask God (29:14)? What does this tell us about the condition of David's heart?

12. What did David know about wealth (29:16)? Compare this to the warning God gave the Israelites (Deuteronomy 8:10–17).

13. What did David know about God (1 Chronicles 29:17)?

    How did David give?

    How did the people give? What does this tell us about the responsibility and opportunity of those in leadership?

14. What did David ask for the people and for his son Solomon (29:18–19)?

15. **Fast forward approximately 250 years:** The kingdom has been divided, the kings have become corrupt, and the prophet Isaiah is speaking for the LORD. Read Isaiah 29:13. What had happened to the hearts of the people and to their worship?

16. **Fast forward to the first century:** Read Mark 7:1–23. Why did the religious leaders criticize Jesus (vv. 1–5)?

What did Jesus say about them (7:6–8)? Whom did He quote?

What didn't the Pharisees understand about the purpose of the law and who it was for (7:9–13)?

What did Jesus tell His disciples was more important: what "goes in" or what "comes out" (7:17–23)?

17. With this in mind, why is it futile to keep trying harder to give joyfully?

18. What does this study teach about the importance of the heart? Why is it important for our desires and actions to be the same?

19. What did God give to express His love for us (John 3:16)?

20. How did God reconcile His love for justice with His love for sinners (Romans 5:8)?

NOTES

IDENTITY
Made in God's Image

Genesis 1:26–28; 2:7; 4:1–16; 9:6; Exodus 31:1–11;
1 Corinthians 12

WHEN I WAS young, I would hold my breath when I couldn't get what I wanted from my parents. Somewhere in my developing psyche must have been the idea that if I couldn't have what I wanted at that precise moment, the rest of my life wasn't worth living. However, I didn't go off to a private place, lie down, stop breathing, and quietly die. I did the opposite. I performed a dramatic scene on the front lawn. I raised my shoulders to expand my lungs, took a deep breath that filled my cheeks as well as my chest, and waited where I knew my mother could see me. My action was more about wanting attention than wanting death.

Recalling my petulant performance makes me wonder whether I do this with God.

Before we explore that possibility, however, let's look at the idea of breath. The word *soul* comes from the Hebrew word *nepes* and the Greek word *psuché*, which mean "breath." It is God's breath in us that defines our "self": "Soul is personal existence . . . the unique personal life, the individual self" (*New International Encyclopedia of Bible Words*).

One dictionary defines *soul* as "the immaterial essence, animating principle, or actuating cause of an individual life." According to the Bible, the animating force within each human being is the breath of God. We are nothing but a clump of dust until God breathes His life into us.

> "[H]uman beings are more than dust. In the creative act, God not only formed the human body but also 'breathed into his [man's] nostrils the breath of life, and man became a living being' (Ge 2:7). Human beings are unique among living creatures, for the life that God created and with which he endowed them is a reflection of his own image and likeness (Ge 1:26). The body may die, but our individual essence will never be dissolved." (*New International Encyclopedia of Bible Words*)

Our souls contain the essence of our identity, so loving God "with all your soul" involves discovering who we are.

1. Read Genesis 1:26–28. What makes humans unique among creation (v. 27)?

LESSON SEVEN: *Identity*

2. What assignments does God give to humans (1:28)?

Read Genesis 2:7. What are humans made from?

What makes humans alive?

Almost from the beginning, poets, playwrights, and philosophers have been asking the question "Who am I?" In Scripture, the question is both asked and answered.

3. The first person to ask an identity question—at least the first that is recorded for us—was known for another first. Who was he and what "first" made him notorious (Genesis 4:1–16)?

What "identity" question did he ask God (4:9)?

What was God's surprising answer? What punishment did God impose?

4. Why is murder such a serious offense? What does it destroy (Genesis 9:6)?

5. Now back to the question raised in the introduction: *Do I ever withhold from God a gift He has given me?* In addition to the very air we breathe, consider the many other gifts we receive from God. List some of them.

Have you ever hoarded a gift from God (as I "hoarded" my breath) and refused to use it for the purpose it was intended? List some examples.

6. The Bible talks about spiritual "gifts," which are given by God to establish His kingdom. One of the earliest references to a

special talent or ability given to an individual is found in Exodus 31:1–11. What "gifts" did God give to Bezalel and Oholiab?

How were the gifts to be used?

7. **Fast forward to the first century:** Several New Testament passages refer to spiritual gifts. One of them is 1 Corinthians 12. To whom are the gifts given (v. 7)?

For what are they to be used (12:7; also 1 Peter 4:10–12)?

8. The apostle Paul used the metaphor of the body to illustrate the way the gifts work together. If you were to think of yourself as a body part, which one would you be? Why?

9. What is your spiritual gift? How are you using it for the common good?

Have you ever considered that you (yes, you!) are one of God's gifts to the world? This means that if you're not being used for the purpose you're here for, it's like holding your breath in God's front yard.

> "In some sense one is given, almost at birth, a song to sing, and part of life, part of the spiritual journey of life, is to look for and listen for that song and then to sing it and live it out." (Don Saliers)

If you're unsure of your spiritual gift(s), your church may have resources to help you determine what it is. Help is also available online. Here are three web addresses.

http://buildingchurch.net/g2s-i.htm
www.mintools.com/spiritual-gifts-test.htm
http://www.churchgrowth.org/cgi-cg/gifts.cgi?intro=1

BROKEN
Lost in Sin

Isaiah 41:14; Malachi 1:2; Romans 7:24; 5:8; Luke 19:10;
Matthew 10:37–39; Ephesians 4:31–32; John 4:1–42

SOME PEOPLE DON'T like to sing "Amazing Grace" because they don't like referring to themselves as a wretch (i.e., "Amazing Grace, how sweet the sound, that saved a *wretch* like me"). And the editors of some hymn books have even changed a stanza of a well-known eighteenth-century hymn to make it less offensive (or, as some would say, to make *us* less offensive). The original lyrics of "Alas! And Did My Savior Bleed?" by Isaac Watts were, "Would He devote that sacred Head for such a *worm* as I?" Many hymn books now read, "Would He devote that sacred Head for *sinners* such as I?"

Frankly, I don't see the big deal. The good news of the gospel is that even wretches and worms can be loved by God and redeemed for a noble purpose. Praise the Lord!

1. Read Isaiah 41:14. What adjective does God use to describe Jacob, whom He loved (Malachi 1:2)?

2. **Fast forward to the first century:** How would the apostle Paul answer the question, "Who am I?" (Romans 7:24)?

    Why does "sinner" sound more acceptable than "wretch" or "worm"?

3. Read Romans 5:8. How did God demonstrate His love for us?

4. Whom did Jesus say He had come to seek and to save (Luke 19:10)?

What then do we need to admit about ourselves before we can be found?

Why is this so hard to do?

5. In the same category as *worm*, *wretch*, and *sinner* is the word *loser*. No one wants to be called a loser. But consider what Jesus said. Read Matthew 10:37–39. What did Jesus say we must lose?

Jesus is not saying that we must all be martyrs (though some will be). The Greek word translated "life" is *psuché,* the same word Jesus used for "soul" when quoting *Shema*. Since "self" is one of the synonyms, consider what verse 39 means if we think of it as losing our "selves," or giving up our identity for Christ's. Read Ephesians 4:31–32. What part of our "selves" are we to "lose" (or "get rid of")?

What characteristics of Christ's "self" are to replace our old selves (4:32)?

With God, being honest about who we are leads to a relationship, not rejection. Jesus proved this in His encounter with a woman of not-so-noble character. Tired from a long journey, Jesus sat down beside a well in a town that most self-respecting Jews would go the extra mile to avoid. Then He started a conversation with a woman no self-respecting Jew would speak to.

6. Read John 4:1–42. What did Jesus ask the woman (4:7)?

Why was the woman surprised (4:9)? What did she know about Jesus? What did she assume about herself?

Instead of giving her a direct answer, how does Jesus respond (4:10)?

LESSON EIGHT: *Broken*

List the steps of the conversation that led up to the point where Jesus disclosed who He was (4:26)

4:11–12

4:13–14

4:15

4:16

4:17

4:18

4:19–20

4:21–24

4:25

4:26

Before Jesus told the woman who He was, He told her some unpleasant truths about who she was. Even though Jesus revealed what the woman surely would have preferred to keep hidden, she headed back to town with a surprisingly positive attitude. What did she say to the people (4:29)?

Why did many of the Samaritans believe (4:39)?

What was the woman's testimony (4:39)?

Why was it so amazing that they would believe her?

7. Have you ever been told an unpleasant truth about yourself in such a kind way that you were actually glad to hear it? Describe the occasion.

8. Imagine having the ability to tell someone the truth about themselves and their sinfulness in such a way that they not only accept it, but welcome it, and run to tell others about it. If more of us had this skill, how might it change our families and our churches?

9. How did Jesus exemplify this statement: "Build a bridge of love that can bear the weight of truth"?

10. Why does denying the truth about ourselves keep us from seeing the truth about God?

> "I came to a point where I couldn't justify what I did, although I knew that it fit who I was as a person and the expression I was longing for. Yet when it came down to looking at this sublime grace that was flowing out of my own hands, I didn't know how to justify it. The more I thought about it, the more depressing it became. I knew that when I was making art it was very rich, very real, very refined and very beautiful. Yet I could not accept that beauty for myself. I knew that inside my heart there was no place to put that kind of beauty. And the more I painted, the more I realized that this schism between what was going on in my heart and what I was able to paint was growing larger. When I finally embraced the faith that there was this presence, this Creator behind the creation, then I had a way to accept this beauty, because I had been accepted by someone even more sublime." (Makoto Fujimura, artist and founder of IAM)

NOTES

REDEEMED
Found in Christ

Exodus 3:13–15; 34:6; *Matthew* 3:17; *John* 6:48; 8:12; 10:11;
11:25; 14:6; *Revelation* 22:13; *Colossians* 1:15–18, 27; 2:9–10;
Acts 17:16–28; *John* 5:19; 15:5; 1 *Thessalonians* 2:11–12;
2 *Peter* 1:3–4; *Ephesians* 1:12; 2 *Thessalonians* 2:13–14;
1 *John* 3:1

THE BIBLE INDICATES that each of us is a unique individual designed by a loving and creative God, equipped with certain talents, fueled by particular passions, to fulfill a specific purpose. But what is our purpose? And how do we find it?

When God announced to Moses that he had been chosen to lead the children of Israel out of Egypt, Moses tried to argue his way out of it by asking the identity question: "*Who am I* to lead these people?" (Exodus 3:11). His response was somewhat disingenuous in that forty years earlier Moses was already thinking of himself as Israel's deliverer. God graciously ignored that detail (see Exodus 2:11–15).

God could have given His reluctant appointee a pep talk about how well equipped he was for the task, but He didn't. He could have recited Moses' life story, reminding him of how he had been spared from death at infancy, reared in the king's palace, and prepared in the sheep fields of Midian to learn—by practicing on sheep—the difficult task of leading difficult people. But there was no "You can do it if you try" talk from God. God was more concerned about Moses knowing who God was than in bolstering Moses' self-confidence.

God chose not to answer the identity question Moses asked. Instead He told Moses what He wanted him to know. In essence He said, "Moses, you're starting with the wrong question. Before you can find out who *you are*, you need to learn who *I am*."

And that is where all questions of identity begin.

1. What did God tell Moses His name was (Exodus 3:13–15)?

2. How did God later expand on His name (Exodus 34:6–7)?

3. Since we are made in God's image, how should we be different than we are? Or, how *would* we be if sin had not destroyed our true identity?

4. **Fast forward to the first century:** Jesus left the comfort and
safety of heaven to put flesh on God's bare-boned answer
to Moses' question "Who are you?" What did God say about
Jesus (Matthew 3:17)?

Jesus expanded on His Father's name by adding details to the
name "I AM." What are they?

John 6:48

John 8:12

John 10:11

John 11:25

John 14:6

Revelation 22:13

5. In the writings of the apostles, God added to the testimony of
His Son, revealing even more about His identity. In a letter to
believers living in Colosse, Paul expanded on Christ's list of
"I ams" with an amazing "He is" list. Who does Paul say Christ
is?

Colossians 1:15

Colossians 1:17

Colossians 1:18

6. In a stunning statement that is nearly lost because it is one of several in the passage, Paul writes: "God has chosen to make known among the Gentiles the glorious riches of this mystery . . ." What is this mystery (Colossians 1:27)?

Consider: People living in that part of Asia believed in mythical gods that were impetuous and impersonal, who hovered above the people, lived in man-made temples, and demanded bloody self-sacrifices from their followers. They had no concept of a God who would come down, make a personal sacrifice, and take up residence in His followers.

7. Later in his letter to believers in Colosse, Paul adds another unheard of idea. Read Colossians 2:9–10. What is "in Christ"? And what have we been given?

One of the mistakes we make in trying to determine God's purpose for our lives is that we reduce it to decisions related to what we should *do*: where we should go to school, where we should live, whom we should marry, what career we should pursue, and what job we should take. Then we compound our faulty thinking by falsely assuming that right choices will lead to fairy-tale endings.

8. Read Acts 17:16–28. Describe the situation in Athens. What pastime characterized the Athenians (17:16–21)?

In modern-day language, we might say that Paul "met the Athenians where they were." What clever appeal did he use to get them to listen to his message (17:22–23)?

What distinction did Paul make between the gods the Athenians knew and the One they didn't? In other words, what made the God Paul worshiped different from all other gods (17:24–26)?

Read verse 28 slowly and thoughtfully. Rewrite the following phrase using first person pronouns (I/my): "In whom we live and move and have our being."

What does it mean to have your "being" in God?

While "what to do" decisions are important, the Bible indicates that they are secondary. The first question each of us must ask is "*Am I* in Christ?" If the answer is yes, the next question is "*Who am I* in Christ?" Regarding this, Jesus made two important statements.

9. Read John 5:19. What surprising admission does Jesus make about himself?

10. Read John 15:5. What important revelation does He make about us?

In a Regent College chapel service, Professor Paul Stevens said, "God has called you, and God is calling you . . . You and I are not left to invent the meaning of our lives. We are not left to figure out what we're on earth for. Or to find out who we are simply by introspection. God has called you into relationship with Himself . . . before we are called to do some*thing*, we are called to some*One* . . . We won't find out who we are without finding out Whose we are. Never forget *Whose* you are, because that is *who* you are."

Lesson Nine: *Redeemed*

11. The apostle Paul elaborated on this calling. Complete the
    following: *We are called . . .*

    into _____ (1 Thessalonians 2:11–12)

    by _____ (2 Peter 1:3–4)

    for _____ (Ephesians 1:12)

    to _____ (2 Thessalonians 2:13–14)

12. Read 1 John 3:1. Who are we?

PURPOSE
Restored for God's Glory

Ephesians 5:1–21; 2:6–22; Matthew 5:9; 2 Corinthians 5;
Genesis 3:7; 1 Peter 2:4–12; Matthew 5:21–26; Romans 15:5–7

IF SALES ARE any indication of need, a lot of people are still trying to answer the question posed by the subtitle of Rick Warren's bestselling book *The Purpose-Driven Life: What on Earth Am I Here For?* In the first year of publication, the book sold more than ten million copies, breaking the sales record for any book previously published. Although record-breaking sales of this book are good news for the author and publisher, they raise a troubling question for the Christian community: Why are so many people so uncertain as to God's purpose for their lives?

For thirty years, the Campus Crusade for Christ booklet "The Four Spiritual Laws" has been a popular tool for evangelism. Law number one is "God loves you and offers a wonderful plan for your life." Why then do so many Christians have such a hard time finding it?

Perhaps we are looking in the wrong places.

Comedian and playwright Woody Allen said, "My one regret in life is that I am not someone else."

What a sad statement. But many of us have felt the same way. An internet search for the phrase "I don't want to be me" turns up hundreds of sites—some of them song lyrics, but many of them the journals of young people lost in a hostile world that assaults them with messages saying they're not good enough.

The desire to be someone other than who we are keeps our economy growing. Marketing mavens capitalize on our dissatisfaction with ourselves by creating the cult of celebrity and using "unreal" people to sell us products we don't need with the promise of illusions that we can't sustain. But we keep trying to make the illusions real, and our failure to do so only deepens our dissatisfaction.

Those who perpetrate this crime against our identity get little attention. We are more bothered by a problem referred to as "identity theft." But identity cannot be stolen. Credit card numbers, bank account numbers, and social security numbers can be taken and used fraudulently. But these do not add up to our identity. We are more than a collection of numbers connecting us to our earthly riches, and anyone who implies otherwise is committing another kind of identity fraud by reducing us to the sum of our bank balances.

A more insidious crime against identity is the one we perpetrate against ourselves. Although our identity cannot be stolen, it can be forfeited. And when we try to be someone other than who we are, we are committing spiritual suicide.

Remember the tenth commandment? "You shall not covet . . . anything that belongs to your neighbor" (Deuteronomy 5:21). This means, of course, that we should not covet our neighbor's talent or intelligence or long legs or thin ankles.

To become like someone else who is already beautiful or popular or talented or intelligent often seems easier than discovering our own gifts and abilities, passions and desires, and finding a place to use them. But what a waste! God doesn't need two of anybody. He needs one of each of us!

1. Think of someone you have tried to emulate—perhaps someone from childhood—who seemed to "have it all," or at least everything that you deemed important at the time. Describe the experience.

Read Ephesians 5:1–21. Who are we to imitate (v. 1)?

What will be the result (5:2)?

How will we be different (5:15–21)?

Consider: The time we spend trying to make ourselves into the image of someone else is time lost in being restored to the image of God.

The well-known hymn "Amazing Grace" uses the phrase "I once was lost but now am found." Ephesians 2 mentions several "was" and "am" conditions. List some of them in the following chart.

I was / You were / We were	I am / You are / We are

2. Read Ephesians 2:6–22. Why did God raise us up (2:6–7)?

By what are we saved (2:8)?

By what are we *not* saved (2:9)? Why not?

LESSON TEN: *Purpose*

What are we saved "to do" (2:10)?

Consider: The Greek word translated *workmanship* in Ephesians 2:10 is *poiema* from which we get the English word *poem*. In other words, *we are* God's poem, His artistic expression. *We are* God's good work!

What "work" does a poem do? In a poem, who is the real "worker"?

Have you ever thought of yourself as God's poem? How does this change the way you see yourself and your purpose?

What was Christ's purpose (2:11–17)? What is He reconciling (v. 16)?

What is Christ creating out of us (2:19–22)?

Why can Christ's purpose not be fulfilled without reconciliation?

3. In Jesus' most famous sermon, He indicated that the children of God are those who *make* peace (Matthew 5:9).

Consider: the nations of the world send peace*keepers* into places where corruption and injustice have led to conflict, strife, and the loss of many lives. Peace*keeping* is defined as "the preserving of peace; *especially* international enforcement and supervision of a truce between hostile states or communities."

Note the use of the word *enforcement*. What does this imply? What kind of "peace" results?

A peace*maker*, on the other hand, is defined as "one who makes peace especially by reconciling parties at variance." How is this different? Why is it more stable?[1]

How did Christ model the role of peace*maker*? How are we to imitate Him?

---

1 For further study see the *Slippery Slope* brochure produced by Peacemaker Ministries. http://www.peacemaker.net/Slippery_Slope

4. Read 2 Corinthians 5. Why is life on earth less than satisfying (5:1–4)? Consider this passage alongside Genesis 3:7. What did we lose at the fall? And what do we try to gain with our own good works?

For what purpose has God made us (5:2–5)?

What motivated the apostle Paul (5:14)?

For whom did Christ die and for what purpose (5:15)?

What work did God do through Christ (5:18)?

What ministry has God given to us (5:18)?

What message has He committed to us (5:19)?

Therefore, who are we (5:20)?

What does God want us to become (5:21)?

5. Read 1 Peter 2:4–12. What is God building (v. 5)?

In the construction business, why is it important that every piece fit? What does this tell us about why reconciliation is essential to God?

Lesson Ten: *Purpose*

What kind of offerings does God want (2:5)?

For what purpose have we been called (2:9)?

What is the purpose of living godly lives in the presence of ungodly people (2:12)?

6. We often think of worship as having three parts: praising God through music, giving of tithes and offerings, and preaching the Word. But Jesus mentions a prerequisite that is seldom included in any worship service. Sandwiched between Christ's teaching on murder and adultery is a troubling paragraph. Read Matthew 5:21–26. What does Jesus say we must do before offering our gifts to God?

Why is this so important to God? Read Romans 15:5–7.

Consider: The world calls for peace in the form of quelling of anger and hostility. Jesus came to bring peace in the form of joyful exuberance for the goodness and generosity of God. The world calls for tolerance; the Bible calls for love. Which would you rather be: tolerated or loved? Why? How does this apply to our lives at home and in the church?

7. Read and reflect on the following quotation. Now think of yourself as God's song or poem (not as a singer or composer or writer or any other "doer"). When you think of yourself as "being" God's good work as opposed to "doing" His good work, what changes?

"Musical harmony softens hard hearts. It induces in them the moisture of reconciliation and it invokes the Holy Spirit. When different voices sing in unity they symbolize the simple tenderness of mutual love. When different voices blend in song they symbolize the blending of thoughts and feelings, which is the highest pleasure human beings can know. Let the sweet sound of music enter your breast and let it speak to your heart. It will drive out all darkness and spread spiritual light to every part of you." (Hildegard von Bingen)

AGREE

What God Wants Us to Think

Romans 12:1–2; Psalm 73:28; 92:1; 100:5; 1 Timothy 2:1–4;
Hebrews 13:9; Psalm 90:14; 145:16; Isaiah 55:1–3; 58:9–11;
Ezekiel 7:19; Esther 5; Mark 15:14–16; Numbers 14:41;
Joshua 1:6–9; 1 Samuel 18:13–16, 28–30; 1 Chronicles 22:13;
Psalm 21:11; 37:6–10; Proverbs 21:30; Daniel 11:36;
Mark 12:30; 1 Corinthians 1:10–25; Philippians 4

ONE NEAR-DEATH experience was all it took to make me change my driving habits forever. It started with an ordinary bike ride. I hopped on my 10-speed and headed down a busy street with a 55-mph speed limit.

When I was about halfway to my destination, I hit a stone in the road, lost control of my bike, and went hurtling headlong across the pavement. Just then a car went whizzing past. If the driver had been passing me as most drivers do—without moving into the passing lane—I would have been road-kill. But he went around me as if passing a car—and by doing so spared my life.

Like I said, the experience changed the way I drive. It also made me passionate about changing the way others drive—particularly my husband. Jay has shown much improvement in this area over the years. One day as we were driving, he moved all the way into the left-hand lane to pass a person on a bicycle.

"Did you notice how I passed that kid on the bike?" he asked. "I did it because I know it makes you happy."

As soon as the words were out of his mouth, I knew that my attempt to protect bike riders had failed. If Jay drives this way only to please me, he probably does it only when I'm in the car.

For years I believed that the highest motive for doing good is the desire to please God. But when Jay's desire to please me left me unsatisfied, I realized that my desire to please God probably doesn't satisfy Him either.

Just as I want something more from Jay, God wants something more from us. Yes, He wants us to obey because we want to please Him (i.e., have the desires of our hearts aligned with His). But more than that, He wants us to obey because we agree with Him about what is good (i.e., have our minds and thoughts aligned with His). That's what I want from Jay. I want him to believe that my way of passing bikers is the safest and best way to drive, not just my paranoid personal preference.

Three words parents long to hear from their children are: "You are right." I think God is waiting to hear those same words from us.

Lesson Eleven: *Agree*

1. Read Romans 12:1–2 from *The Complete Jewish Bible* (below).

> "I exhort you, therefore, brothers, in view of God's mercies, to offer yourselves as a sacrifice, living and set apart for God. This will please him; it is the logical "Temple worship" for you. In other words, do not let yourselves be conformed to the standards of this world. Instead, keep letting yourselves be transformed by the renewing of your minds; so that you will *know* what God wants and will *agree* that *what he wants is good, satisfying* and *able to succeed.*" (italics added)

What does the author exhort us to do?

What is the basis for his appeal?

What are we to avoid?

What must happen *in* us to avoid having this happen *to* us?

What does God want us to know?

What does He want the result of our knowledge to be?

2. Without looking in a dictionary, write a definition of good.

3. What does God say is good?

Psalm 73:28

Psalm 92:1

Psalm 100:5

1 Timothy 2:1–4

Hebrews 13:9

How does your definition of good compare to what God says?
What can you do to get your thoughts about goodness aligned
with God's?

4. Make a list of things that people think they need to be satisfied. Personalize the list by putting a check mark by the items that, at one time or another, you thought you needed to be satisfied.

5. What does God say about satisfaction?

   Psalm 90:14

   Psalm 145:16

   Isaiah 55:1–3

   Isaiah 58:9–11

   Ezekiel 7:19

6. The Old Testament tells the sad story of a man who could not be satisfied without getting revenge. Read Esther 5. Why did Haman hate Mordecai (5:9, 13)?

7. The New Testament tells the sad story of a man who looked in the wrong place for satisfaction. Read Mark 15:14–16. Who did Pilate want to satisfy?

8. Think of a time when you did something you knew was wrong to appease (or satisfy) someone else? How did it turn out? Was the person satisfied?

9. What do we risk when we try to please ourselves apart from God? What do we lose when we seek satisfaction from anyone other than God?

10. Without looking at a dictionary, write a definition of success.

11. What does God say about success?

    Numbers 14:41

Joshua 1:6–9

1 Samuel 18:13–16

1 Samuel 18:28–30

As you read the passages from 1 Samuel, reflect on the differences between David and Saul in regard to their attitude about success.

1 Chronicles 22:13

Psalm 21:11

Psalm 37:6–10

Proverbs 21:30

Daniel 11:36

12. Little has been written as to why Jesus added "mind" to *Shema* (compare Deuteronomy 6:4–5 and Mark 12:30). However, in Paul's first letter to the church in Corinth he gives a clue. Read 1 Corinthians 1:20–25. Much of the New Testament was addressed to a Gentile audience, primarily those influenced by the Greeks. To the Greeks, the mind was the center of life. In contrast to the Jews, what did Paul say the Greeks were looking for (v. 22)? What does Paul say about wisdom?

13. As the seeds of the gospel were sown outside the land of Israel, some took root in thorny places where paganism had long been the prevailing belief. In places where people believed in many gods, there was little agreement as to what was good, satisfying, or able to succeed. Thus disagreement was a serious problem in the early church. Read 1 Corinthians 1:10–17. Summarize the dilemma Paul was addressing. What was his appeal to believers (v. 10)?

14. Read Philippians 4:1–9. Describe the problem alluded to in verse 2. What did Paul plead for?

15. How were others to help in making this come about (4:4–7)?

16. What "mental antidote" does Paul give for disagreement (4:8–9)?

17. If everyone were in agreement with God as to what is good,

satisfying, and able to succeed, what would happen to disagreements between one another?

18. Following are some verses with the phrase "are right." Choose one that is pertinent to your situation, look it up in your Bible and read it in context, then meditate until you have some helpful insight. Write a brief statement or prayer about what you have learned.

The whole assembly responded with a loud voice: "**You are right**! We must do as you say." (Ezra 10:12)

Righteous are you, O LORD, and **your laws are right.** (Psalm 119:137)

All the words of my mouth are just; none of them is crooked or perverse. To the discerning all of them **are right**; they are faultless to those who have knowledge. (Proverbs 8:8–9)

Who is wise? He will realize these things. Who is discerning? He will understand them. **The ways of the LORD are right**; the righteous walk in them, but the rebellious stumble in them. (Hosea 14:9)

"Well said, teacher," the man replied. "**You are right** in saying that God is one and there is no other but him. (Mark 12:32)

They all asked, "Are you then the Son of God?" He replied, "**You are right** in saying I am." (Luke 22:70)

Jesus said to her, "**You are right** when you say you have no husband. The fact is, you have had five husbands, and the man you now have is not your husband. What you have just said is quite true." (John 4:18)

"But if I do judge, **my decisions are right**, because I am not alone. I stand with the Father, who sent me." (John 8:16)

"You are a king, then!" said Pilate. Jesus answered, "**You are right** in saying I am a king. In fact, for this reason I was born, and for this I came into the world, to testify to the truth. Everyone on the side of truth listens to me." (John 18:37)

REMEMBER
What God Wants Us to Recall

Deuteronomy 6:8–9; Genesis 9:16; Exodus 20:8;
Deuteronomy 4:9; 5:15; 6:12; 8:11; 2 Kings 17:38; Proverbs 4:5;
Isaiah 46:9; Nehemiah 9:17; Psalm 106; Exodus 17:8–15;
Deuteronomy 25:17–19; 1 Samuel 15; Esther 1–10

AT A SUMMER art fair I found a pin featuring the faces of characters from *The Wonderful Wizard of Oz*.

Dangling beneath the face of the friendly but Cowardly Lion is a yellow star with the words "Be Brave." Beneath the hollow stare of the Tin Woodman dangles a red heart with the words "Have a Heart." And beneath the mindless expression of the Scarecrow is a turquoise circle with the words "Use Your Brain."

The artist was memorializing L. Frank Baum's childhood classic, but to me the pin symbolized what Jews call *Shema*, and what Jesus called the Greatest Commandment.

In the Tin Woodman who finally feels emotion, I saw a symbol of loving God with my heart. In the Scarecrow who learns that he can think, I saw a symbol of loving God with my mind. And in the

Cowardly Lion who finds courage, I saw a symbol of loving God with my strength. So I bought the pin to wear as a reminder to love God as He loves me—with heart, mind, and strength—all working as one for the good of all.

Think of an object that you keep because it reminds you of something you don't want to forget. As you work on this study think of a symbol (memory device) that will help you remember something you've learned in this study. If you are studying in a group, take the symbol to your next meeting.

In an earlier lesson we alluded to some ancient memory devices. When Moses addressed a throng of recently freed slaves, he emphasized the importance of the commandments he was about to give by also giving these instructions to aid in remembering them: "Tie them as symbols on your hands and bind them on your foreheads. Write them on the doorframes of your houses and on your gates" (Deuteronomy 6:8–9). Throughout Scripture we often find God "showing" us how to live rather than just telling us. This is one of those times. Long before this command was given God indicated that He too uses memory devices.

1. Read Genesis 9:16. What memory device did God use? What does it help Him remember?

2. For the most part, God told the Israelites to remember good things. Read the following passages and summarize what they say about remembering.

   Exodus 20:8 (another example of God *demonstrating* how to live rather than just telling us)

   Deuteronomy 4:9

   Deuteronomy 5:15

   Deuteronomy 6:12

   Deuteronomy 8:11

   2 Kings 17:38

   Proverbs 4:5

   Isaiah 46:9

3. Despite repeated reminders to remember what God had done for them and had called them to do and be, the people of Israel forgot. Read Nehemiah 9:17. What were the consequences of not remembering?

4. Read Psalm 106. Pay special attention to verses 7, 13, 21, 45

and their immediate context. What does the song say about the consequences of not remembering?

5. There is one notable exception to the positive nature of the things the Jews were to remember. Read Exodus 17:8–15 and Deuteronomy 25:17–19. What "bad" thing did God tell the Jews to remember (25:17)? Why (25:18)?

Fast forward several hundred years: Israel's King Saul was informed that he was to be God's partner in carrying out this plan. God sent Saul and his army to punish the Amalekites for attacking Israel when she was so vulnerable and when God had made it so clear that He was involved in her escape from Egypt. God instructed Saul to "totally destroy everything" that belonged to the Amalekites, not sparing women, children, or even livestock (1 Samuel 15:1–3). According to Deuteronomy, Amalek was singled out for such harsh punishment because the nation "did not fear God" (25:17–19).

Saul started the battle well. He summoned 200,000 foot soldiers and 10,000 men from Judah, "went to the city of Amalek and set an ambush in the ravine" (15:6). But he did not end it well. Saul took King Agag alive, and the army also spared "the best" of the livestock. They were willing to totally destroy only that which was "despised and weak" (15:8–9). God was not pleased with Saul's partial obedience and He spoke these startling words: "I am grieved that I have made Saul king, because he has turned away from me and has not carried out my instructions." When God was grieved so was Samuel, and he cried out to the Lord all night (15:10–11).

After the battle Saul claimed to have carried out the Lord's plans. When questioned by Samuel, Saul rationalized his choice by claiming that he kept the best for a sacrifice to God. Samuel knew this was nonsense. God had already said what he wanted from Saul, and it was obedience, not a fancy sacrifice. Saul apparently thought more highly of himself and his own plans than of God and His plans.

Samuel spoke harshly to Saul: "Does the LORD delight in burnt offerings and sacrifices as much as in obeying the voice of the LORD? To obey is better than sacrifice, and to heed is better than the fat of rams. For rebellion is like the sin of divination, and arrogance like the evil of idolatry. Because you have rejected the word of the LORD, he has rejected you as king" (15:22–23). Saul immediately acknowledged his disobedience. "I have sinned," he said. But the next words out of his mouth indicate that he didn't hear the accusation of arrogance: "But please honor me before the elders of my people and before Israel."

6. **Fast forward approximately 500 years:** Read Esther 3:1–6. Whom did King Xerxes honor and what was the man's ancestry (3:1)?

7. What enraged Haman (3:2–4)? In regard to desire, how was Haman like some other biblical characters we have studied? (Hint: consider what he had, as opposed to what he didn't

have.) What does Haman's desire tell us about what he believed about himself?

8. What was Haman's solution for getting rid of his rage (3:5–6)?

9. Read Esther 4:1–14. What strong words did Mordecai use to convince Esther to intercede before her husband on behalf of her people the Jews (4:12–14)? What did Mordecai say would happen if she refused (4:14)? What does this tell us about God's dependence on Esther? What did Mordecai suggest was the purpose for Esther's rise to royal position (4:14)?

10. Read Esther 5. Consider Esther and her husband, King Xerxes. She knew about his love for partying. Did she use this knowledge for good or evil (5:1–8)? Explain.

11. Consider Haman and his wife, Zeresh: She knew about his

desire for self-aggrandizement. Did she use this knowledge for good or evil (5:9–14))? Explain.

12. How do you use your knowledge of other people? To influence them for evil by encouraging them to use their weakness as an opportunity to sin? Or to influence them for good by turning their weakness into an opportunity to blot out evil?

13. Read Esther 6. What did Haman think (6:6)? What miscalculation did he make based on his wrong thinking? How does Haman exemplify Proverbs 16:18?

14. Haman's wife and advisers, who once encouraged Haman in his evil plot to elevate himself, have changed their minds in regard to the outcome. What "encouraging" words do they offer Haman (6:12–14)?

15. The ending of this episode of Jewish history is a classic case of

poetic justice. What happened to Haman (Esther 7:10)? What happened to Mordecai (10:1–3)?

16. In celebration of this miraculous turn of events, the Jews established an annual holiday. A party called Purim has become their memory device. Read Esther 9:20–32. What and why did they celebrate (9:22a)? How did they celebrate (9:22b)?

All religious holidays are memory devices. The celebration of Purim reminds us that God is still in the business of blotting out evil and every memory of it.

Fasting is another form of remembrance. Giving up food doesn't make us more spiritual, but it does make us think differently about food. Fasting from a meal or from a certain food is not evidence of our goodness; it's an acknowledgment of God's goodness, for it causes us to remember that God provides all good things. It also reminds us that "no one is good—except God alone" (Mark 10:18).

17. What symbol or memory device did you come up with as suggested at the beginning of this lesson? What does it help you remember?

18. Read the following quotation and follow the instructions in the last sentence:

> "Memory is essential to being human. Commemoration acknowledges and honors God's saving acts among us. The past is not obsolete or irrelevant. We do not invent the life of faith; we come to a dynamic and personal faith within the context of the traditions our spiritual ancestors have shaped and preserved for us. What have you inherited from your spiritual forebears? Thank God for their faithfulness. Make a list of what you would like your children or some future generation to remember about your spiritual life." (*The Spiritual Formation Bible*, p. 652)

Consider: The only good reason to remember an evil act is to remind ourselves that God is working to obliterate evil and He has chosen us to help.

Consider: There will be no tears or sorrow in heaven because God finally will have accomplished His purpose of blotting out the memory of every evil thing done by us and to us.

BELIEVE
What God Wants Us to Know

Exodus 6:1—8; 7:1—5; 29:44—46;
Jeremiah 9:23—24; 23:16—17; Ezekiel 6:7, 10, 13, 14; Psalm 78;
Luke 12:42—48; John 1:1—9; 6:25—40; 6:1—15; 14:9—14; 17:20—23;
16:12—15; 20:31; Colossians 3:2; Hebrews 3:1; Genesis 18:10—15;
Mark 5:25—34; John 21:14—18; Luke 17:3—4

THE WAY SOME people talk, you could get the idea that faith is
nothing more than a spiritualized form of wishful thinking. The slogan
"Just Believe" decorates everything from sweatshirts to wall hangings
to Christmas cards and ornaments. But the kind of faith these
advocate has more to do with the mystical power of positive thinking
than anything God ever said on the subject.

Although it doesn't do much good to talk back to a slogan, I'd
like to ask, "Believe what?" Believe that God will repay money we
foolishly borrow? Believe that God will neutralize the consequences
of all our bad choices? Believe that God will give us the car, career,
or spouse of our dreams if we promise to behave in a certain way?

Contrary to what we'd like to believe, faith is not convincing ourselves that we have God's stamp of approval on our plans; it's believing that God's plans are better than ours.

That's what Noah believed, and so, at God's instruction, he set about building a houseboat to save himself, his family, and a remnant of the animal kingdom from the flood God said was coming, even though Noah had never seen a drop of rain.

That's what Abraham believed, and so, at God's command, he left the comfort and familiarity of home and headed across the desert for a place God said was better, even though Abraham had never seen it.

That's what Moses believed, and so, by faith, he refused the privileges rightfully his as the son of Egypt's ruler and identified himself instead with people God said He had chosen for himself, even though they were still slaves belonging to Pharaoh.

Biblical faith is not about taking risks; it's about taking on the identity of Jesus. It's not about having the audacity to do what is foolish; it's about having the courage to do what is difficult. It's not about running in the dark; it's about walking in the light. It's not about believing what people say about God; it's believing what God says.

Lesson Thirteen: *Believe*

1. Read Exodus 6:2–3. This passage indicates that God did something for Moses that he did not do for Israel's patriarchs Abraham, Isaac, and Jacob. What was it (6:3)? What does this indicate about God's plan for making himself known?

2. What does God promise to do *for* the Israelites (6:6–7a)? What was God's purpose in doing this (6:7b)?

3. Read Exodus 7:1–5. What does God promise to do *to* the Egyptians (7:3–4)? For what purpose (7:5)?

4. Read Exodus 29:44–46. What did God want the Israelites to know (29:46)?

5. Read Jeremiah 9:23–24. What is the only legitimate reason for boasting? If you had to rate your right to make this boast—on a scale of 1 (low) to 10 (high)—what would your score be? What can you do to improve your score?

6. Read Jeremiah 23:16–17. Why is it important for everyone, not just professional clergy, to know God's truth?

7. In her book *When Life and Beliefs Collide*, Carolyn Custis James confirms the importance of women having knowledge and theological understanding:

> "[A] woman's interest in theology ought to be the first thing to catch a man's eye. A wife's theology should be what a husband prizes most about her. He may always enjoy her cooking and cherish her gentle ways, but in the intensity of battle, when adversity flattens him or he faces an insurmountable challenge, she is the soldier nearest him, and it is her theology that he will hear. A woman's theology suddenly matters when a man is facing a crisis and she is the only one around to offer encouragement." (p. 51)

Recall Esther and Zeresh from lesson 12. How did their theology (i.e., their beliefs about God) affect the advice they gave their husbands? How do your beliefs about God affect your marriage, your family, your work, your life?

8. Read Ezekiel 6:7, 10, 13, 14. Write the phrase that is common to all these verses.

9. Fifty-nine times in the book of Ezekiel a variation of the phrase "will know that I am the Lord" appears. Most of them refer to some form of desolation or destruction that God is going to use to prove to the world who He is. This was not God's "Plan A." His original plan was to make himself known through His goodness to the Israelites and to the rest of the world through the Israelites. But this plan was foiled by disbelief (see for example Psalm 78:32; for a poetic history of Israel, read the entire Psalm). Pause for a moment and think of other things— perhaps in your own life—that were (or may have been) foiled by disbelief.

10. **Fast forward to the first century:** Read this familiar verse: "From everyone who has been given much, much will be demanded." Without looking it up in your Bible, write down what you think the first "much" refers to.

Now look it up and read it in context: Luke 12:42–48. After

reading it, would you answer the question differently? If so, how? What does it tell us about God's plan for making things known? What does it imply about the level of responsibility for people living in our century?

What will happen to those who are entrusted with knowledge but use it for their own gain (12:46b)?

11. The gospel of John uses the word *believe* more than any other book in the Bible. Read John 1:1–9. John claims to have been sent from God for a specific purpose. What was it (1:7)?

12. Read John 6:25–40. What is the work of God (6:29)? What do you think Jesus meant?

What "follow-up" question did the people ask (6:30–31)? Consider their question in light of what they had experienced the previous day (6:1–15). What does this tell us about how difficult it was for the people to believe? And what does it imply about the value of "experiential" evidence?

13. Read John 14:9–14. What did Jesus want His disciples to believe (14:11)?

14. Read John 17:20–23. What does Jesus want the world to believe (17:21)? How will this be accomplished?

15. Read John 16:12–15. What did Jesus say the Holy Spirit would do? What does this tell us about the human capacity to comprehend truth and God's plan for disclosing truth?

16. What was John's purpose for writing his gospel (John 20:31)?

17. In what place are we to "set our minds" (Colossians 3:2)? What do you think this means?

18. In a passage of Scripture that we commonly refer to as the Lord's Prayer, Jesus makes a statement that we often repeat without engaging our minds. He said, "your will be done on earth as it is in heaven" (Matthew 6:10). Have you ever asked yourself, "How is God's will done in heaven?" Think about this question and write down your thoughts. Then ask yourself, "How can we do God's will on earth without first finding out how God's will is carried out in heaven?"

19. What happens when you think too much about "earthly things"? List some examples.

20. When you're in love, what do you think about? Read Hebrews 3:1. On whom are we to "fix our thoughts"? What difference would doing this make in your interactions with others and in the way you spend your time?

21. Scripture memorializes two women for their thoughts. One has become an example of doubt, the other of faith. Read Genesis 18:10–15. Describe Sarah's thoughts about God (18:12).

Read Mark 5:25–34. Describe this woman's thoughts about God (5:28).

How were the two women alike? How were they different?

Ironically, the wife of the man known as "the father of faith" (Romans 4:11–13) is remembered for her doubt. Sarah didn't believe that God could fulfill a promise which experience told her was impossible. In contrast, the anonymous woman whom Mark writes about, even after twelve years of going from doctor to doctor only to get sicker and poorer, had the faith to believe that Jesus could do for her what doctors could not. Instead of building her belief system on the foundation of her own disappointing experiences, she built it on her knowledge of the proclamations of ancient Jewish prophets who predicted that the Messiah would come as a healer.

Which of the two are you more like? Do your experiences

determine what you believe about God? Or does your knowledge of God determine how you interpret your experiences? Has the answer changed over the years? Describe the process.

22. Read John 21:15–18. What is the most important thing that God wants to know about us?

23. Read the following passages, paying special attention to the bold type. What is remarkable about them?

"As the heavens are higher than the earth, so are my ways higher than your ways and **my thoughts than your thoughts**." (Isaiah 55:9, emphasis added)

He who forms the mountains, creates the wind, and **reveals his thoughts to man**, he who turns dawn to darkness, and treads the high places of the earth—the Lord God Almighty is his name. (Amos 4:13, emphasis added)

We do, however, speak a message of wisdom among the mature, but not the wisdom of this age or of the rulers of this age, who are coming to nothing. No, **we speak of God's secret wisdom, a wisdom that has been hidden and that**

LESSON THIRTEEN: *Believe*

God destined for our glory before time began. **None of the rulers of this age understood it**, for if they had, they would not have crucified the Lord of glory. However, as it is written: "No eye has seen, no ear has heard, **no mind has conceived what God has prepared for those who love him**"—but God has revealed it to us by his Spirit.

The Spirit searches all things, even the deep things of God. For who among men knows the thoughts of a man except the man's spirit within him? In the same way **no one knows the thoughts of God except the Spirit of God. We have . . . received . . . the Spirit who is from God, that we may understand what God has freely given us**. This is what we speak, not in words taught us by human wisdom but in words taught by the Spirit, expressing spiritual truths in spiritual words. The man without the Spirit does not accept the things that come from the Spirit of God, for they are foolishness to him, and he cannot understand them, because they are spiritually discerned. The spiritual man makes judgments about all things, but he himself is not subject to any man's judgment: "For who has known the mind of the Lord that he may instruct him?" **But we have the mind of Christ.** (1 Corinthians 2:6–16, emphasis added)

After meditating on this question and these passages, write a prayer or journal entry about what this means to you.

Strength
Take Courage

Joshua 1; Isaiah 40:26—31; Luke 1:11—13, 26—30; 2:8—14;
Matthew 8:28—34; Luke 1:31—38, 46—53; Matthew 14:22—36;
1 Corinthians 10:23—31; 2 Corinthians 12:7—10;
Ephesians 1:18—21; 3:14—19; 2 Timothy 1:7; 2:1;
Colossians 1:9—14; 3:12—17, 23—24; John 14:19—20;
Romans 12:9—21

ON THE MORNING of September 11, 2001, I had just finished reading the book of Esther for my devotions when I learned what was happening in New York City.

I didn't immediately see the relationship between the events that I'd just read about and those that I was watching on a small screen in my living room. But as the day's events unfolded, I realized that the story of the Persian queen was like a 2500-year foreshadowing of the day we will always remember as 9/11.

The book of Esther tells the story of a young Jewish orphan who became queen of Persia (much of which is now Iraq and Iran). But her privileged life was interrupted when a beloved family member announced that the fate of all her relatives—thousands of people—depended on her willingness to risk her life by confronting her ruthless husband.

After fasting and praying for three days, Esther accepted the challenge and risked her life by appealing to the king, who then spared the lives of all the exiled Jews living in the Persian Empire.

As I listened to the stories of the phone calls made by people on United Airlines Flight 93 that crashed in Pennsylvania, I thought, *That plane must have had some Esthers on board. They heard the call, recognized their duty, and risked their own lives to save others.*

Then I thought, *If God had people on board that plane to thwart the enemy, why would He not have had people in other strategic places who could have stopped the evil of that day before it grew to such tragic proportions?*

Based on what I know about the character of God, I believe He did. I think God had people stationed at all kinds of intersections along the way, who, for one reason or another, turned their heads, didn't want to be inconvenienced, and refused to believe that anything bad would happen if they ignored "potential" evil. How could anyone have known that taking the easy way would lead to death for so many innocent people? How could they have known that ignoring a small suspicion would result in evil on a scale that the Western world seldom sees?

This leads to more personal questions: How much evil do we ignore in ourselves because we refuse to believe that our anger, self-indulgence, or stubbornness will ever hurt anyone, or will ever get so big that we can't control it? And how much evil do we ignore in other people because we lack the courage to try to stop it, or because we don't want anyone to dislike us, or because we don't want to be inconvenienced?

LESSON FOURTEEN: *Strength*

As I witnessed the unfolding drama of 9/11, I saw my purpose in a new light. As Mordecai said to Esther, "Don't think you're here simply for your own pleasure and enjoyment; you're here to stand with God against evil."

As believers in Christ, we are called to this same task. And to accomplish it we need strength and courage to stomp on Satan's head when evil slithers into our lives.

With this lesson we start circling back to the beginning because our study of strength leads back to a matter of the heart—the emotion we refer to as fear. The phrase "do not [or "don't"] be afraid" is used 89 times in the NIV translation. And in several places it's linked to the concepts of strength and courage.

1. Read Joshua 1. Circle the phrases that have to do with strength and courage. Where do strength and courage come from (1:6–9)?

2. Read Isaiah 40:26–31. What does the prophet say about strength?

3. **Fast forward to the first century:** In the gospels, the words "do not be afraid" frequently are spoken by angels. The most common response to messengers from heaven is fright. Read Luke 1:11–13, 26–30, and 2:8–14. These passages do not support the stereotype that angels are comforting creatures whose presence brings calm. What do they imply about human ability to recognize what is from God?

4. Demons, in contrast, seem to be considered a part of everyday life. The people of that day apparently acknowledged that they had no power over them and simply did their best to maintain a "peaceful coexistence" by trying to avoid them and trying not to disturb them. Read Matthew 8:28–34. Summarize what happened. How did the people respond? Why do you think they pleaded with Jesus to leave their region?

Think of other examples of evil that we tolerate simply because we don't want to stir up trouble for ourselves or someone else. What would be a better response?

5. Return to Luke 1 and read verses 31–38. Imagine that you are

Mary trying to digest the news that you have just heard. List some of the implications of this news for Mary's future. What uncertainties did it create for her? How did she respond (1:38)? What kind of courage did it take for her to answer in such a way? Would you have had the courage to answer the way Mary did?

Read Luke 1:46–55. What did Mary know about God that gave her such courage? (1:50–55). What did Mary say that God knew about her (1:48)?

6. Several years later, Mary's grown son had chosen His disciples and had become a popular teacher. Read Matthew 14:22–36. What words did Jesus use to calm his frightened friends (14:27)?

Unlike the words spoken by the LORD to Joshua ("Be strong and courageous"), Jesus said to the disciples "Take courage." Where do you think they were supposed to "take courage" from?

The Greek word translated "It is I" [Eijmiv]□ is the same word that is translated "I am." If the disciples heard Jesus say "I am," what would they immediately think of?

7. Read 2 Corinthians 12:7–10. In his second letter to believers living in Corinth the apostle Paul writes about the paradox of power. In what is power made perfect (12:9)?

Verse 10 describes attitudes that do not come naturally. Have you been in a situation when you were genuinely able to delight in weaknesses, insults, hardships, persecutions, or difficulties? If so, summarize the experience.

8. Read Ephesians 1:18–21. What does Paul pray for?

How does he describe the "incomparably great power" that he wants us to know [i.e., what is the power like?] (1:19–20)?

LESSON FOURTEEN: *Strength*

9. Read Ephesians 3:14–19. What does Paul say the power of God should be used for (3:18–19)?

10. In writing to Timothy, what spirit did Paul say that we have *not* been given (2 Timothy 1:7)?

11. In what are we to be strong (2 Timothy 2:1)?

12. Read Colossians 1:9–14. What does Paul say about the reason we need strength and power (1:11)?

In studying the section on strength, I learned that the word translated "might" or "strength" in *Shema* (Deuteronomy 6:5) is used not as a noun to refer to physical strength or bodily power but as an adverb to describe intensity. One lexicon defines it as "a marker of great degree or quantity: very, greatly, exceedingly, much" (H4394 *Hebrew English Lexicon of the OT Law*).

In a sense, therefore, "strength" is not the last in a series of ways to love God but the exclamation point at the end of the command.

Another way of saying it might be "Love God with all your heart, with all your soul, with all your mind, and love Him so intensely in all these areas that no competing desire, motive, or thought can find a place within you to take root."

One New Testament passage says the same thing in another way. In his first letter to believers living in Corinth, Paul addressed the problem of how to observe religious practices about which the people disagreed. The controversy in this case had to do with whether or not believers should eat food that had been offered to an idol.

13. Read 1 Corinthians 10:23–31. What ungodly desires might have led to the conflict?

What ungodly motives might have fueled the conflict?

What ungodly thoughts might be thriving in the conflict?

14. Instead of saying whether the practice was right or wrong, and instead of giving guidelines for *making* the decision, Paul gave

them a principle to govern whatever they decided. What was it (10:31)? And how might it settle the conflict?

15. Think of a contemporary conflict and fill in the blanks:
So whether you _____ or
_____ or whatever you do, do it all for the glory of God.

16. Read Colossians 3:12–17. What is the "super glue" of virtues (3:14)?

17. Read Colossians 3:23–24. The word translated "heart" in verse 23 is *psuche*, a word we looked at in an earlier lesson. It means "breath" and it's more often translated "life" or "soul." Rewrite the verse substituting these three words for "heart."

18. Whenever evil rears its ugly head in the form of some obvious atrocity like mass murder or a terror attack, the world asks,

"Where is God?" Christians don't have to ask that question because Jesus told us where God is. Where does Jesus say that God is (John 14:19–20)?

We can ignore people who ask, "Where is God?" We can shrug our shoulders and even join those who ask it. Or we can say, "Here He is, living in me. In the power of Christ, I'm not afraid to stand against evil."

That's what Ashley Smith did. On Friday, March 11, 2005, the spotlight of national media attention focused on an accused rapist who gunned down a judge and other law enforcement officials in an Atlanta courtroom. He escaped from the building before anyone could stop him. A search began immediately, and cable news stations carried all-night live coverage.

The next morning, after his capture, media attention quickly turned away from the criminal and onto the woman credited with bringing the crisis to a peaceful end.

"God brought him to my door," headlines quoted her as saying. Who was this woman who would give God credit for bringing an accused rapist and murderer to her door?! We'll never know how many lives Ashley saved when she recognized that being held hostage by an accused rapist and a murderer was really a divine appointment. She probably didn't think of herself as a courageous person. But she knew where to get courage when she needed it. She reached out and took it from the One who said, "Do not be afraid, I AM."

It's unlikely that any of us will ever find ourselves in circumstances like hers. Most of our life situations are far less dramatic—but perhaps no less important.

LESSON FOURTEEN: *Strength*

The apostle Paul made a bold and puzzling statement in his letter to believers in Rome. He said, "Do not be overcome by evil, but overcome evil with good" (12:21). This sounds rather simplistic until you consider what precedes it.

19. Read Romans 12:9–21. Which of these is easy for you to do?

In these verses Paul tells us *how* to overcome evil with good! The behaviors he mentions are the good with which God will overcome evil. And when you think about it, they all require strength and courage.

We never know when a small act of courage—perhaps something as simple as honoring one another above ourselves or being patient in affliction—will have eternal consequences. Choose one of the phrases from this passage that is relevant to something happening in your life. Write a prayer asking God for the strength to overcome evil with good in this situation.

Consider: Loving God with all my strength involves more than filling my calendar with charitable activities or checking off a list of good deeds. It means daily doing right in little things that are difficult so that when a "big" opportunity comes along I'll have the confidence to believe that God, through me, can accomplish it.

Loving God with all my strength means having the courage to risk my "self" for the sake of what God says is true and right and good.

AFTER THE FALL
Finding the Strength to Get Up

Job 32—37; Romans 12:3; Job 42; John 20:23; Romans 14;
Isaiah 45:20; 46:1; Luke 11:46; Matthew 11:26—30; Isaiah 57:13;
Ephesians 5:21; 1 Peter 5:5—6; Philippians 2: Isaiah 64:6;
James 4:10; Revelation 1:12—18; Jude 1:17—25

A TEEN-AGE GIRL in our neighborhood walks dogs for their owners. Sometimes she walks several at a time. I should say she "*tries to* walk them." Each dog has its own agenda, its own speed, and its own set of expectations as to the purpose of a walk. One thinks the purpose is to be first, so it's out in front trying to pull the others along. One thinks its purpose is to investigate, so it tugs to go sniff a tree. One thinks it's to "enlarge its borders," so it stops every few steps to mark its territory. One is convinced that moving left is best, so it tugs in that direction. Another is sure that right is the better way to go and pulls in that direction. Soon the leashes become entwined and the dogs start nipping at each other. The girl has to stop and straighten them out before they can proceed. Not far down the road the process repeats itself.

When I watch the girl trying to manage the disorderly dogs, I wonder if God ever feels the way she must feel. Like the Israelites before us, Christians sometimes behave like a pack of dogs on leashes. Each of us uses all of our own strength to go our own way. As a result, the pleasant journey God mapped out for us is disrupted by conflict.

One of my favorite Peanuts comic strips features Charlie Brown saying to Snoopy, "I hear you're writing a book on theology. I hope you have a good title." Snoopy responds, "I have the perfect title: *Has It Ever Occurred to You That You Might Be Wrong*?"

The question in Snoopy's title is best used when each of us asks it of ourselves.

A character in the book of Job certainly would have been better off if he had asked himself Snoopy's question.

1. In Job 32–37 we read the discourse of Elihu, the fourth of Job's so-called friends or comforters. Read all six chapters if you have time. If not, read Job 32:1–10. Why was Elihu angry with Job (32:2)? And with his three friends (32:3)?

2. Read Job 32:17–22; 33:1–3, 31–33. How would you describe Elihu? What does he promise to deliver (33:33)?

LESSON FIFTEEN: *After the Fall*

3. The more Elihu talks the more worked up and arrogant he
   becomes. Read Job 36:1–4. What does Elihu think of himself
   (36:4)? Elihu of course did not have the advantage of reading
   Paul's letter to believers in Rome. But we do. What did Paul
   write that can help us avoid Elihu's error (Romans 12:3)?

4. Every time I read the book of Job I want to cheer when I get
   to chapter 38 and God finally speaks for himself. What does
   God have to say about those who have been speaking on His
   behalf (38:2–3)?

5. Read Job 42:1–17. How did Job respond after being
   questioned by God (42:6)?

   Why was God angry at Eliphaz and his two friends (42:7)?

   What did God tell them to do to avoid having Him deal with
   them according to their folly (42:8)?

If you were Job, how would you feel about having to pray
for your three friends after the unfair judgments and false
accusations they had made against you? Read John 20:23.
How do the words of Jesus fit Job's situation? How do they fit
yours?

What happened to Job after he prayed for his friends (42:10;
also see 12–17)?

What did Job's friends finally admit about the source of Job's
trouble (42:11)? What did Job finally receive from his friends
(better late than never!)?

I once decorated a notebook with definitions of the words *idea*,
thought, *opinion*, *preference*, *belief*, and *conviction* to remind myself
that they are not synonyms and that I need to beware of elevating my
ideas, thoughts, and opinions to the level of beliefs and convictions.

6. Read Romans 14:1–4. On what are we *not* to pass judgment
(14:1)? Why not (14:4)?

7. Read Romans 14:13–19. Instead of passing judgment, what are we to do (14:13, 19)?

Furthermore, we need to subjugate even our beliefs and convictions to the law of love, which leads to peace and mutual edification and which transcends all other laws. Whenever our own opinions and preferences become more important to us than what God says is true, important, and valuable, we have made them into idols, and we have become idolaters.

Idolatry is the most serious offense in the Bible because it violates the first and most important command: "You shall have no other gods before me" (Exodus 20:3). An idol is more than a carved or forged image. It's a symbol of everything that the god stands for (or, in most cases, that we "fall for").

As I read the Bible I'm amazed by all the trouble people go to to create and care for their own gods—gods that are worse than helpless; they're needy!

8. Turn to the book of Isaiah. What does God say about those who carry idols (45:20)?

How does the prophet describe idols (Isaiah 46:1)?

9. **Fast forward to the first century:** For what did Jesus chastise the teachers of the law (Luke 11:46)?

10. What did Jesus say about His "burden" (Matthew 11:26–30)? What makes you weary? What are you carrying that you were never meant to carry?

11. Read Isaiah 57:13. What is the difference between those who worship gods they have made and those who worship the God who made them?

False gods fall over and have to be set upright. They have to be carried from place to place (or washed or cleaned or put away; or, in the case of opinions and preferences, defended). They are a burden. But people would rather cater to the gods they create than bow down to the One who created them. They would rather "own" a god they can set upright than allow the God who owns them to set them upright. People work tirelessly to appease false gods but refuse to do the one thing that will make them acceptable to the One true God: bow down.

Over the centuries, the entrance to Bethlehem's Church of the Nativity has twice been made smaller. (The purpose in the most recent renovation was to keep marauders from entering the basilica on horseback.) The entrance now is referred to as the Door of Humility because visitors must bend down to enter.

As we age, bending our knees becomes increasingly difficult and painful—both physically and spiritually.

In the physical realm, some people courageously undergo knee replacement surgery. To avoid years of increasing pain and debilitating joint damage, they endure several weeks of agony.

Like physical knees, spiritual knees become stiff over time. Years of stubborn pride and self-centeredness make us inflexible, and it becomes increasingly difficult and painful for us to humble ourselves. Seduced by false feelings of importance when others submit to us, we never learn that true importance comes from submitting ourselves to God and others (Ephesians 5:21; 1 Peter 5:5).

The Door of Humility at the Church of the Nativity reminds us that we all need new knees—knees that will bend. The replacement procedure is painful, but it's the only way to enter the presence of God.

12. Read Philippians 2:5–11. What is the attitude of Christ that we are to emulate (2:5–8)?

What did God do for Jesus because of this attitude (2:9)?

What will the rest of the world one day do (2:10–11)?

13. Using the familiar verse Romans 3:23, preacher and author John Piper defines sin as "falling short of the glory of God." Sinfulness then is the condition of having lost the glory of God as our covering. Realizing that we are naked is important, but it doesn't solve our problem; it only makes us vulnerable to those who are in the business of fabricating and selling the latest fashions in self-righteousness. What does the prophet Isaiah say about self-righteousness (Isaiah 64:6)?

14. Read 1 Peter 5:5–6. With what are we to clothe ourselves (5:5)? Why?

What will happen if we humble ourselves (5:6)? When?

15. Read Revelation 1:12–18. What happened when John heard a

LESSON FIFTEEN: *After the Fall*

voice behind him (1:12)? Who did he see (1:13–16)? How did
he respond (1:17)?

16. Read James 4:10. What are we to do? Why?

In an earlier lesson we learned that the only real strength any of
us have is God's. In this lesson we see that the only official act
of strength God asks that we perform "on our own" is to humble
ourselves. In doing so, we learn the solution to the basic human
problem stated in Lesson 1: "I've Fallen and I Can't Get Up." We now
know that . . .

The only way to get up is to bow down!

NOTES

LOVING GOD WITH all my heart, soul, mind, and strength means that I am continually repenting of desires, motives, thoughts, and habits that alienate me from God.

Sometimes we think of repentance as a once-in-a-lifetime event, as though once we turn to God for salvation there's no more turning to be done. But for the Christian, repentance is a way of life. As God deepens our understanding of himself and His purpose for our lives, we turn away from our old ways of thinking, behaving, and judging. Daily we bow down and humbly submit ourselves to the desires, purposes, and practices that God has ordained for each of us.

Repentance becomes a way of life as we come to understand the pattern of God's relationship with humanity: *revelation, alienation, reconciliation.* The pattern started with Creation, the Fall, and the giving of the Law. It continued in the Incarnation, the Crucifixion, and the Resurrection. And it keeps repeating itself in individual lives on a daily basis. God gives us life and breath, sunshine and rain, food and flowers, sunsets and sunrises, friends and family. Yet we are constantly enticed to pursue things that look nicer, smell sweeter, or promise something better.

Jesus said, "The time has come. The kingdom of God is near.

Repent and believe the good news!" (Mark 1:15). When we surrender our preconceived ideas about what is right and turn away from the illusions that entice us to pursue ever-changing desires, we will no longer be lured into situations where we become victims of ever-changing passions.

NOTE TO THE READER

The publisher invites you to share your response to the message of this book by writing Discovery House Publishers, P.O. Box 3566, Grand Rapids, MI 49501, U.S.A. or by calling 1-800-653-8333. For information about other Discovery House publications, contact us at the same address and phone number.